Science
WORKBOOK

Author **Lynn Huggins-Cooper**

KS2

VISUAL REVISION GUIDE

SUCCESS

CONTENTS

CONTENTS

Green plants need water, light and the right temperature to grow properly. If you leave a green plant in the dark for a few days, it will begin to go yellow and look sickly as it cannot make food. It needs the energy from the sun to make food in its leaves.

If you do not water a plant enough, it will soon go brown and dry up. Leaves will drop off and eventually the plant will die.

not enough light

healthy plant

not enough water

GROW UP!

Q1 Look at these statements. If they are true, write T in the box. If they are false, write F.

a Plants need light and darkness to grow. F

b Plants need light and water to grow. T

c Plants can turn black if they are put in the dark. F

d Plants can turn yellow if they are put in a dark place. T

e Plants can dry up and go brown if they do not have enough light. F

f Plants can dry up if they do not have enough water. T

Q2 Imagine you are growing some daisies in a pot. Tick where you would put the pot to make sure they get enough light.

a Under the bed. ☐

b On a light shelf. ☑

c In a dark cupboard, under the stairs. ☐

d In a dark shed. ☐

Q3 Complete this crossword.

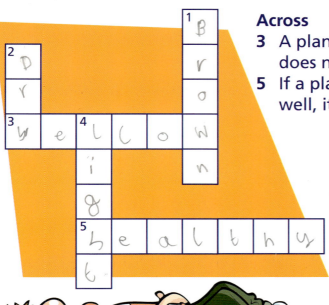

Across

3 A plant goes this colour if it does not get enough light.

5 If a plant is green and growing well, it is described as this.

Down

1 A plant goes this colour if it does not get enough water.

2 A plant goes this texture without enough water.

4 As well as the right temperature and water, plants need this to grow.

Crossword answers:
- 1 down: Brown
- 2 down: Dry
- 3 across: yellow
- 4 down: Light (licon?)
- 5 across: healthy

Hi! My name's Sam. I've got a bossy sister, called Mel. Funny thing is if I turn the light off in her room, she goes green – not yellow! Draw a plant in the space below that has not had enough light. What would it look like?

Challenge

BRAIN TEASER

See how much you can remember! Imagine you are writing an article for the school magazine. Make a list of instructions for someone trying to grow plants and keep them healthy.

1. Put on window sill
2. Water every 12 hours
3. check it every 6 hours
4. DO Not let it turn brown or yellow

When a seed starts to grow, we say it has <u>germinated</u>. Seeds need water and the right temperature to germinate. Some seeds need light, too. First, a tiny white root grows down. Then a tiny shoot grows up. This happens whichever way up you plant a seed! The shoot will develop tiny leaves.

Seeds are spread in many ways.

in the air

by animals

by birds

by water

The different parts of a plant each have a job to do. The leaf uses sunlight to make food. The stem takes water and goodness to different parts of the plant. The roots anchor the plant securely in the ground and help it to take up water from the soil. If flowers are bright and smell nice, the plant needs insects to <u>pollinate</u> it. If it has feathery flowers and no fragrance, it is probably pollinated by the wind.

PLANT POWER

Q1 Look at these statements. If they are true, write T in the box. If they are false, write F.

a Seeds need water to germinate.

b Acorns are seeds, that grow into oak trees.

c The green beans we eat with our dinner are seed pods.

d When a seed starts to grow, we say it has generated.

e Seeds need water and the right temperature to grow.

Q2 Complete these sentences using the words in the box.

root   germinated   pollinated   water   sunlight

a   The _____ holds a plant in the soil.

b   Leaves make food using _____.

c   The stem of a plant takes _____ and goodness from the roots to other parts of the plant.

d   If flowers are bright colours and smell good, the plant is probably _____ by insects.

e   When a seed starts to grow, we say it has _____.

Q3 Match the seed to the description of how it is spread.

a   I move by floating on water.

b   I have a feathery parachute that blows on the wind.

c   I spread as the fruit is eaten by birds.

d   I have hooks that catch in the fur of animals.

dandelion seed

coconut

holly berry

burr

SCIENCE FACT
Some seeds actually need a period of very cold weather before they can germinate. Gardeners sometimes keep seeds in the fridge for a while before they plant them to make them germinate!

Hello!
I'm Mel. I think my pesky younger brother, Sam, often looks seedy, but he never drifts off, worst luck! Draw three pictures in order, to show how a plant grows from a seed to an adult plant.

Challenge

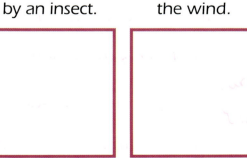

BRAIN TEASER

1 Draw a plant that would be pollinated by an insect.

2 Draw a plant that would be pollinated by the wind.

When you want to sort a group of things, you look for things that are the same and things that are different about members of the group. A crab, a snail, a butterfly and a ladybird could be sorted into groups in the following ways.

| Crab and snail = has shell | Butterfly and ladybird = does not have shell | OR | Butterfly and ladybird = has wings | Crab and snail = does not have wings |

Scientists sort animals and plants into lots of different groups. An example would be birds, reptiles, insects, fish and flowering plants. A spider would come under insect.

SORT IT OUT!

Q1 Sort these creatures into the two groups below.

alligator mouse fish snake bird

Has scales	Does not have scales

SCIENCE FACT

Have a look at this great website to take part in some interactive classification activities: www.hhmi.org/cool science/critters/critters.html

Q2 Draw these creatures in the correct group. Be careful, some of the creatures are members of both sets!

snake alligator hen kestrel turtle butterfly penguin bat

lays eggs   lays eggs and can fly   can fly

Which creatures are members of both groups or sets?

_____

Q3 Which group does each animal or plant belong to? Tick the correct box.

a crocodile ☐ bird ☐ reptile ☐ insect ☐ fish ☐ flowering plant

b daffodil ☐ bird ☐ reptile ☐ insect ☐ fish ☐ flowering plant

c seagull ☐ bird ☐ reptile ☐ insect ☐ fish ☐ flowering plant

d beetle ☐ bird ☐ reptile ☐ insect ☐ fish ☐ flowering plant

Challenge

I tried sorting Mel and her friends into sets but they all squeal, they all giggle too much ... I couldn't find any differences at all!
Look at this list of living things and think of at least four ways to sort them into sets.

eagle owl tiger lion
turtle rabbit ladybird

BRAIN TEASER

How could you sort these creatures into groups? Think of how they are similar or different to each other. Write your group titles in the circles, then draw the animals in the correct circle.

ladybird duck grasshopper penguin

9

IT'S ALIVE!

How can we tell if things are alive? All living things, creatures and plants, do things that tell us they are alive. We call these things the seven life processes.

These life processes are:

Movement
Growth and change
Reproduction (have babies)
Respiration (breathing)
Sensitivity (feel things)
Nutrition (feeding and eating)
Gets rid of waste.

All seven processes need to be present before something can be said to be alive.

Sometimes it's hard to see all these things happening! For example, plants don't breathe in the same way as humans, but they do take in and give out gases. This is a type of respiration, just like breathing. We can't usually see plants moving, either. They do move though, when they grow towards the light.

Q1 **Which of these things prove that something is alive? Tick the boxes.**

a It shines and glitters. ☐

b It moves. ☐

c It breathes. ☐

d It makes a noise. ☐

e It feeds. ☐

f It falls over. ☐

g It feels things. ☐

h It squashes easily. ☐

i It produces babies. ☐

j It grows and changes. ☐

k It gets rid of waste. ☐

Q2 **Look at these statements. If they are true, write T in the box. If they are false, write F.**

a Trees are alive, because they show all seven processes of life. ☐

b A river is alive, because water moves and makes a noise. ☐

c A hurricane is alive, because it makes a loud noise. ☐

d Cats are alive, because they move, feed and produce babies. ☐

e Plants are alive, even though we can't see them moving. ☐

f All living things reproduce. ☐

Q3 **Circle the things in this picture that are alive.**

SCIENCE FACT

The important thing to remember is that to be living, all seven life processes must take place. Just making a noise and moving do not count! Think of waves, streams and flames. They are all noisy and move, but they are not alive.

Well, you wouldn't think Sam was a living thing, as he's always lazing about with his headphones on, doing nothing and showing no signs of life! Try drawing a picture of each life process. Careful though, the descriptions are hard!

Respiration
Reproduction
Nutrition
Sensitivity
Movement
Growth and change
Getting rid of waste

Challenge

BRAIN TEASER

Fill in the missing words to complete the sentences.

1 All living things _____, even plants, although they have no lungs!

2 All living things get rid of _____.

3 Living things all _____ and change.

4 _____ things all need to feed.

11

We say some materials are natural. That means we can find them in the environment. Stone, wood, wool in the form of a fleece, and feathers are natural, for example. Plastic is not natural. It is made in factories. We say it's made by people or synthetic. Be careful though, it can be tricky! Plastic is often made from oil, which is a natural resource. All synthetic materials are made of raw materials.

natural

synthetic

NATURAL OR SYNTHETIC?

Q1 Natural or made by people? Put these materials in the correct group.

wool   plastic   wood   stone   glass
chalk   feathers   metal   polystyrene

Natural

Made by people

Q2 Match the natural material to the thing it is made into. Join them with a line.

a Sheep's wool

b Clay

c Sand

d Iron ore

e Wood

china bowl

steel nail

chair

jumper

glass window

Q3 Fill in the spaces to say which thing from the box was made from these raw materials.

woollen coat   china mug   glass vase   carved chair   ring

a Gold – a precious metal dug as ore from the ground. _____

b Clay – sticky material like mud dug from the ground. _____

c Wool – from a sheep's fleece. _____

d Wood – from a tree. _____

e Sand – dug from quarries and heated to a very high temperature. _____

SCIENCE FACT

A real diamond is a natural thing. It comes from the earth. But scientists can make synthetic diamonds in a laboratory by copying how a real diamond is formed. It is very difficult to tell which is real and which isn't.

I like natural things and kindly fill Mel's bedroom with them! You'd think she'd be grateful, but no! All she does is scream. What harm can spiders, slugs and snails do? They are all natural!

Now look round your house and make a list of ten natural and ten synthetic things. Do you know what natural materials they are made from?

Challenge

BRAIN TEASER

Draw a circle round the natural materials below.

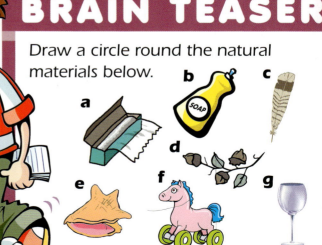

THE ENVIRONMENT

Have you ever walked along the beach and seen lots of rubbish where the tide comes in and out? Or have you seen plastic bags and bottles left behind in the woods after someone's picnic? It looks horrible, but it's also dangerous for wildlife. Rubbish lying around like this is called litter.

Birds can get tangled in fishing lines left on the beach and they cannot escape. In the countryside, bottles can become traps for small animals that can climb in but can't escape. We should try to find ways to reduce the amount of rubbish we throw away. We should also try to reuse things. Bottles, paper and cans can all be recycled. So can some plastics.

We use over 6 billion glass bottles and jars in the UK each year, and every day 80 million drinks and food cans are thrown away. These things could be recycled!

Q1 **Use the words in the box to fill in the gaps.**

discarded   urban   recycled   rubbish

a Litter is _____ left lying around in the environment.

b Birds can get tangled in _____ fishing line.

c Bottles left on the ground after picnics can trap mice and shrews. They should be taken to a bottle bank to be _____.

d Rubbish is not only a problem in the countryside. It is also a problem in _____ areas.

SCIENCE FACT

Why not check the Waste Watch site on the Internet at www.recyclezone.org.uk/school-k/kids.htm. There are great activities to do, including a quiz that tells you how much of a 'waster' you are! You can also make a worm composter for the garden. Your teacher may like to arrange a visit from Cycler the rapping robot!

14

Q2 Look at the scene below. Draw a circle round all the litter you can see. Then make a list of the items and think of ways they could be reused.

_____

_____

_____

_____

_____

Q3 Look at the things in the bin below. Which could be recycled in glass, paper or can banks? Which could be put in a compost heap?

a Glass bank: _____ _____

b Paper bank: _____ _____

c Can bank: _____ _____

d Compost heap: _____ _____

I reused an old football shirt to make cloths for cleaning the hamster cage, but Sam wasn't very pleased!

How could you reuse netting bags that come free with soap powder tablets?

Challenge

BRAIN TEASER

Sort this rubbish into groups.

comic   lemonade can
cottage cheese pot   bean tin
glass milk bottle

Reuse   Recycle

_____   _____

_____   _____

_____   _____

A habitat is the place where a creature or plant lives. Your garden is a habitat. There are lots of plants and even animals to be found in a garden. You find creatures in one habitat that you may not find in another. Creatures develop and change over time to fit their habitat. We call this adaption, because the plants and animals have adapted to suit their environment.

THERE'S NO PLACE LIKE HOME

Q1 Circle the creatures below that would not be found in a garden in the UK.

Name two more animals that you might find in a garden in the UK.

a _____

b _____

Q2 Draw a line to match the creature to the place in the garden where it lives.

a wall   **b** pond   **c** flowerbed   **d** leafpile

Q3 Draw a line to match the animals to the descriptions of how they are suited to their habitat.

a I have a big sticky 'foot' that helps me to stick to surfaces. This means I can travel up vertical surfaces and find food easily! I need to live in a damp place such as under leaves or stones to keep me moist.

b I have a big paddle shaped tail that helps me to swim. I am greeny-brown, which helps me to stay hidden in the pond weed.

c I have a long curled tongue to poke into the centre of flowers so I can drink nectar. My wings help me to fly about so I can reach the nectar!

Mel says she loves wildlife, but you should see her run when there's a big, hairy spider in the bath!

I like woodlice best. I love their armour-plated skin. They look like tiny dinosaurs! They like to live in damp, dark places. Whereabouts in the garden would I find them?

Challenge

BRAIN TEASER

Imagine you are a squirrel. Now describe your habitat.

_____

_____

_____

_____

_____

_____

We have bones for three reasons.

To protect the important, soft parts inside our bodies. Our skulls protect our brains, and our ribs protect soft internal organs like our lungs and heart. The backbone protects the spinal cord.

To give us support. Without bones, we would find it hard to stand up because we would be all floppy!

To help us move about. Our muscles work with our bones to help us walk, bend and lift things.

The place where two bones meet is called a joint. Our elbows, knuckles and knees are all examples of joints.

Many animals, called vertebrates, also have muscles and bones that do the same jobs for them as our muscles do for us. Animals without backbones are called invertebrates.

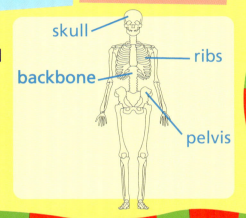

skull

ribs

backbone

pelvis

RATTLE THOSE BONES!

Q1 **Complete the sentences by using the words in the box.**

support   bones   joints   muscles   invertebrates

a _____ help to protect the soft organs inside our bodies, such as our hearts and lungs.

b Your bones _____ your body, and allow you to stand up and move.

c _____ work with bones to help us to move about.

d Animals with backbones (or spines) are called vertebrates. Animals without backbones are called _____.

e Knees and knuckles are examples of _____.

Q2 Draw a line to match the picture of the bones to the job they do.

a Protects the lungs and heart, and other soft organs inside the chest.

b Helps us to bend and stand upright.

c Protects the brain from injury.

d Protects soft organs such as intestines – part of your digestive system.

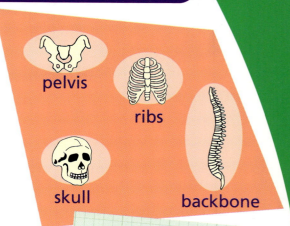

pelvis

ribs

skull

backbone

Q3 Label this skeleton, using the words in the box.

skull backbone ribs pelvis kneecap

a

b

c

d

e

SCIENCE FACT

Bones are alive! They are full of cells. That is how they are able to knit back together after they have been broken.

You have 206 bones in your body.

There are 26 bones in your backbone alone!

Challenge

Sam loves showing off his muscles. Shame they're so tiny! My mum told me that muscles always work in pairs. She said that when he bends his arm, one muscle gets shorter and fatter. It pulls on the bone in the lower arm that it is attached to. At the same time, the other muscle relaxes, getting longer and thinner.

Feel your muscle as you bend your arm. Can you feel the muscle on the top getting fatter? Now relax your arm and feel the muscle again. Describe what you think is happening .

BRAIN TEASER

Write down what each of these words mean or describe, and give an example.

1 Vertebrates _____

_____

_____

_____

2 Invertebrates _____

_____

_____

_____

19

FACTS TO GET YOUR TEETH INTO

We use our teeth to cut and chew our food. Teeth help us to break down food so that our digestive system (such as our stomach and intestines) can get the nutrients (goodness) out of our food.

Some animals, called carnivores, only eat meat – that is, other animals. They have sharp canine teeth that allow them to hold and kill their food. They need teeth that are able to tear tough meat. An example of a carnivore would be a cat.

Other animals, called herbivores, eat only plants. They need incisor teeth for cutting and cropping plants, and molar teeth for grinding them so the plants can be swallowed and digested. An example of a herbivore would be a rabbit.

We should clean our teeth in the morning and before we go to bed to get rid of any bits of food left behind after we eat. The bacteria in our mouths break down food into sugars that make plaque. This is what causes tooth decay.

canine teeth

cat's skull

incisors

molars

rabbit's skull

Q1 Use the words in these boxes to complete these sentences.

incisors   carnivores   decay   herbivores   chewing   canines

a We use our teeth for biting and ＿＿＿＿＿＿＿＿ food.

b ＿＿＿＿＿＿＿＿ are the teeth at the front of the mouth.

c Animals who eat only meat are called ＿＿＿＿＿＿＿＿.

d ＿＿＿＿＿＿＿＿ are the sharp teeth used to tear food such as meat.

e Plaque can cause tooth ＿＿＿＿＿＿＿＿.

f Animals who eat only plants are called ＿＿＿＿＿＿＿＿.

Q2 Look at these statements. If you think they are true, write T in the box. If you think they are false, write F.

a Eating too many sticky sweets is good for our teeth. ☐

b Plaque does not cause tooth decay. ☐

c Carnivores eat only vegetables. ☐

d Herbivores eat only plants. ☐

e Herbivores have sharp canines for tearing meat. ☐

f The bacteria in our mouths break down food into sugars that make plaque. ☐

Q3 Label these teeth. Then describe the job each type of tooth does.

☐
☐
☐

SCIENCE FACT

If you do not look after your teeth, the strong white outer coating of your teeth, called enamel, can get damaged. If you get a hole in the enamel, the acids in your mouth can get to the softer inside layer of your tooth, called dentine. If the acid reaches the nerve at the centre of your tooth – ouch! Toothache time!

a Canine _____

b Incisor _____

c Molar _____

My rabbit uses its long incisors to munch lettuce. Mel likes lettuce and I think she looks a bit like Flopsy, only not so cute and fluffy!

Why does my dog have sharp canine teeth?

Challenge

BRAIN TEASER

1 Why do sheep have large molars?

_____
_____

2 Why do humans have sharp canines and large molars?

_____
_____

Our bodies are mainly made of water, so we need to drink plenty of water to stay healthy. We also need to eat lots of different types of food. Look at the types of food below that we should include in our diet.

Fresh vegetables contain fibre, which we need to keep our digestive system healthy. They also contain lots of vitamins and minerals.

Butter and cooking oils contain fats. These give you lots of energy and can be stored by your body to use as energy later.

Pasta, cereal and wholemeal bread contain carbohydrates, which give us lots of energy that our bodies can use easily. Our bodies burn them to keep warm!

Cheese, eggs, soya, milk, meat and nuts contain protein, which helps our bodies to grow and repair themselves. Dairy products like cheese, milk and yoghurt also contain lots of calcium, which we need to keep our bones and teeth healthy and strong.

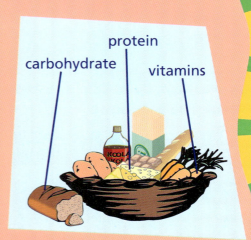

DINNER IS SERVED

Q1 Draw two foods from each group in the boxes.

carbohydrates	vitamins and minerals

fat	fibre	protein

22

Q2 Answer these questions.

a Why do we need to drink lots of water?

_____

b Why should we eat plenty of fruit and vegetables?

_____

c Why do we need to eat foods containing calcium?

_____

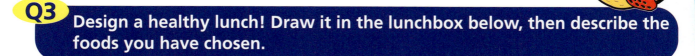

Q3 Design a healthy lunch! Draw it in the lunchbox below, then describe the foods you have chosen.

Why are they healthy foods? Which food groups have you used? What jobs do each food group do to keep us healthy? Use a separate piece of paper if you run out of space here.

_____

_____

_____

_____

SCIENCE FACT

We should eat at least five portions of vegetables and fruit each day to stay healthy. A banana or an apple is one serving, but so is half a cup of cooked vegetables, a cup of salad or a mini box of raisins!

I eat lots of fruit every day. I like making fruit salad best. Sam says he hates my cooking, but my fruit salad keeps disappearing ... and I don't think it's the hamster sneaking out for a snack!

Make up a recipe for a fruit salad. How can you make it as tasty as possible?

Challenge

BRAIN TEASER

A balanced meal is a meal that contains different food groups. You need quite a lot of carbohydrates, some protein, a little fat, vitamins and minerals, and plenty of fibre and water. Plan a healthy menu including a main course, a dessert and a drink. You may need an extra sheet of paper to write on.

_____

_____

_____

_____

23

Blood carries oxygen, heat and the goodness from our digested food round our bodies. The heart acts like a pump that pushes blood round the body. It uses tubes called veins and arteries to move the blood to all parts of the body. Arteries carry blood away from the heart, and veins carry it back.

Blood contains many microscopic cells. Red blood cells carry oxygen around the body that is picked up as the blood travels through the lungs. They carry carbon dioxide, a waste gas, back to our lungs and we breathe it out. White blood cells fight bacteria and viruses that enter our bodies. Blood also contains tiny pieces called platelets. These help our blood to clot when we are cut, so our skin forms a protective layer, called a scab!

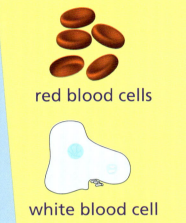

red blood cells

white blood cell

BUSYBODY BLOOD

Q1 Use the words from the box to complete the sentences.

platelets   pump   microscopic   bacteria   arteries   veins

a The heart pushes blood round the body like a _____.

b The tubes that carry blood around our bodies are called _____ and arteries.

c _____ help the blood to clot.

d _____ carry blood away from the heart.

e White blood cells fight _____ and viruses that enter our bodies.

f Blood contains _____ red and white cells.

Q2 Look at these statements. Write T in the box for true and F for false.

a The heart pushes blood around the body.

b Red blood cells fight any bacteria that enter our bodies.

c White blood cells fight any bacteria that enter our bodies.

d Platelets make us bleed.

e Red blood cells carry oxygen round the body.

f White blood cells carry oxygen round the body which is picked up as the blood travels through the lungs.

Q3 Exercise makes our hearts beat faster. Look at the graph below. It shows the changes in Sam's heartbeat as he walks to the park, plays football and then sits down for a drink. Mark the point on the graph to show when Sam sat down for a rest.

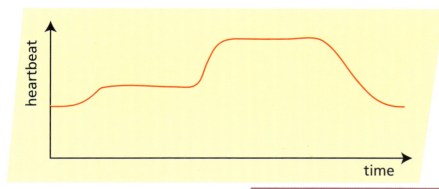

heartbeat

time

SCIENCE FACT

The heart beats more than 2.5 billion times in an average lifetime! You can see an amazing animation of a heart pumping blood on the Internet at:

www.innerbody.com/anim/heart.html

BRAIN TEASER

Draw a line to match the part of the blood to the job it carries out.

red blood cell   white blood cell   platelet

1 Transports oxygen, waste gas, and dissolved nutrients from food round the body.

2 Helps blood to clot.

3 Fights bacteria and viruses that cause disease.

I'd like a vampire bat as a pet! Then we'd see exactly how fast Mel's blood is pumped round her body! Can you think of a way of finding out how fast your heart is beating?

Challenge

25

Have you noticed how things change as they grow? Some creatures just seem to get bigger, with their young (the scientific name for babies) looking like small adults. Humans and dogs are good examples.

Other animals change completely as they grow. Baby ladybirds don't look anything like adults. They are black and scaly, and have no wings. Baby toads – tadpoles – don't look anything like their parents! When animals change completely as they grow, we say they have gone through metamorphosis.

MIGHTY METAMORPHOSIS

Q1 Circle the animals that go through metamorphosis.

a

b

c

d

e

f

g

h

Q2 Draw a series of pictures in a life cycle to show how a frog changes as it grows. Use the words in the box to help you.

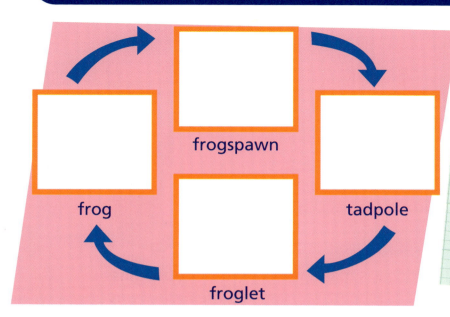

frogspawn

frog

tadpole

froglet

SCIENCE FACT

Many pond creatures and sea creatures, go through metamorphosis. Have a look in a nature book from the library and see how many you can spot. You may be amazed when you see some of the pictures of the babies of familiar animals. They almost look like tiny aliens!

Q3 Draw a series of pictures in a timeline to show how a human grows from a baby to an adult. Then add the letters from the box below to your pictures.

a I am an elderly person. I am a grandma!   **b** I am a teenager
c I am a baby – I am only six months old!   **d** I am an adult – and a mum!
e I am a toddler – I am two years old.   **f** I am a little girl.

I wish Sam would go through metamorphosis, but I suppose he is already a bit of a toad ... ! Can you suggest two more animals that go through metamorphosis, which are not mentioned on this page?

Challenge

BRAIN TEASER

Write a list of four animals, not mentioned on this page, that do *not* go through metamorphosis, so their babies look like small versions of the adults.

1 _____
2 _____
3 _____
4 _____

A material is what an object is made from. Sometimes, people get confused and think that materials just means fabric (the things clothes are made from). Wood, metal, plastic, glass, stone and fabric are all materials.

In your home, you will find many different materials. They are chosen for different jobs because of their properties.

A door could be made from wood, because wood is strong. But a door made from paper would be useless, because it would tear and get soggy when it rained!

A window is made from glass, because glass is transparent. You can see through it and light can travel through it. A window made from stone would be useless, because it would not let in light and you could not see through it!

MATERIAL MAYHEM

Q1 **Look at the descriptions of the properties of different materials. Choose the best material to make each item. Match them with a line.**

a Fabric – soft, easy to cut into different shapes.

b Glass – transparent (see through) – light can travel through.

c Cardboard – light, quite strong – good for making packaging.

d Stone – hard, strong.

e Plastic – light, easy to mould into different shapes when heated.

walls

box

doll

trousers

window

Q2 Suggest the best material to make each item.

a cooking pan _____

b jumper _____

c magazine _____

d doll _____

e paving stones _____

Q3 Put the objects in the box in the correct group.

glass   cardboard   clear plastic ruler   water   milk
mirror   clear plastic bag   wooden tray

transparent   opaque

_____   _____
_____   _____
_____   _____
_____   _____

I told Mel that I would like a chair made of glass – it would look like a throne and she could be my servant! She laughed and said she would sing in a high voice until my chair shattered!

Can you think of a reason why the following things would not be a good choice of materials?

A fabric door.

A bed made from stone.

A window made from paper.

Challenge

BRAIN TEASER

Have a look round your house. Choose an object and explain why it is made from the material it is made from.

_____
_____
_____
_____

29

THAT MAKES A CHANGE!

Materials can be sorted into three groups: liquids, solids or gas.

Liquids flow and change shape to fit the container they are held in. Think of the way milk can be poured from a jug into a glass.

Solids do not flow or change shape in the same way. Think of a block of wood.

Gases also flow and change shape, but they spread out to fill a space, even a space as big as a room!

burp

Oxygen is a gas found in air. We can't see it, but we need it to stay alive. To imagine how a gas spreads out to fill a space, think of the way you can gradually smell something such as perfume.

Materials can be changed from one state (solid, liquid or gas) to another by cooling or heating. Some of these changes are reversible. That means the material can be changed back. Other changes are irreversible. That means they cannot be changed back.

Q1 **Complete the sentences by adding the words *solid*, *liquid* or *gas*.**

a Stone is a hard, strong _____.

b Milk is the _____ babies drink.

c The air we breathe is a _____.

d Balloons that float are often filled with a _____ called helium.

e Clay is a pliable _____ before it is baked hard in a special oven called a kiln.

f Water is a clear, colourless _____. We are mostly made from water!

Q2 How have these materials changed? Write solid, liquid or gas.

a Chocolate is a _____.

When it is heated it changes into a _____.

b Steam is a _____.

When it is cooled, it changes into a _____.

c Water is a _____.

When it is frozen, it turns into a _____.

These are all reversible changes.

Q3 Reversible or irreversible change? Write the correct word in the box.

a Chocolate melting, changing from a solid to a liquid. _____

b Ice melting, changing from a solid to a liquid. _____

c Egg cooking, changing from a liquid to a solid. _____

d Water boiling, changing from a liquid to a gas. _____

e Butter melting, changing from a

solid to a liquid. _____

I love cooking, but Sam says my cooking is *yucky!* I won't offer him any of these pancakes I'm making then! Can you make a list of four foods in the kitchen that change state and can't be changed back?

Challenge

BRAIN TEASER

Fill in the missing words. Use *solid*, *liquid*, or *gas* to fill the gaps. Mel is making pancakes.

1 She weighs out flour and sugar. The flour and sugar are _____.

2 Her mum melts some butter in a pan. It changes from a _____ to a _____.

3 Mel breaks an egg into some flour, and adds milk. The egg is a _____.

4 Mel puts the mixture in the hot pan. It changes from a liquid to a _____.

Sound travels in invisible waves through the air. We can't see these waves, but we can hear them! Sound happens when air is compressed, or moved quickly. Things sound loudest the closer we are to the thing making the noise. We hear things as sound enters our ears. The sound makes our eardrums vibrate and we hear the vibration as sound. Sound is measured in decibels (dB) and is measured by an oscilloscope.

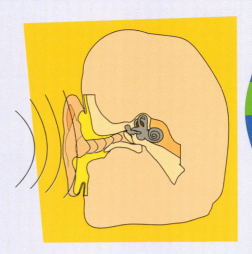

Very loud sounds can damage your ears. This is why you see people wearing earmuffs when they are working with loud tools and machinery. Ears can also be damaged by infections, or by the eardrum being damaged as it is poked, so never put anything in your ears!

SOUND CHECK

Q1 **Complete the sentences by choosing the correct word from the box below.**

waves   vibrations   sound   eardrums   decibels

a We hear _____ when noise enters our ears.

b Sound travels through the air in _____.

c Sound makes our _____ vibrate.

d We hear the _____ as sound.

e Sound is measured in _____.

Q2 Look at the picture below. Where would the noise from the stereo be loudest?

Give a reason for your answer. _____

_____

Q3 How can ears become damaged?

a _____

b _____

c _____

Q4 What can people do to muffle sound if they are using loud machinery?

_____

_____

SCIENCE FACT

An oscilloscope is a special machine used to measure sound waves. It translates noise into a picture we can see on a screen.

I love being noisy!
Make a collage picture of loud and quiet things by cutting pictures out of magazines. Is it easier to find noisy things or quiet things?

Challenge

BRAIN TEASER

Think of four really noisy things that your ears need to be protected from.

1 _____

2 _____

3 _____

4 _____

LET THERE BE LIGHT!

Light travels in straight lines. It cannot bend round objects in its way. This is how shadows are made. An opaque object blocks the light and the shadow shows where the light has been blocked.

Your shadow is roughly the same shape as you, but sometimes it is long and sometimes it is short. This is because of the height of the sun overhead. At midday, when the sun is directly overhead, your shadow is quite short. Late in the afternoon, as the sun is going down, your shadow is much longer.

Light helps us to see things. The light comes from light sources, bounces off objects and enters our eyes.

Q1 Look at these statements. Write T against the ones that are true and F against the ones that are false.

a Light travels in wiggly lines, just like sound.

b Light travels in wavy lines and can bend round corners.

c Shadows are made when an object blocks the light.

d Opaque objects let light pass through.

e Transparent objects block the light.

f Late in the afternoon, shadows are short.

g Late in the afternoon, shadows are long.

Q2 Look at the picture of the cat in the flowery hat. Draw the cat's shadow as it would look in the late afternoon.

a Explain why the shadow looks this way.

_____

_____

b How would the shadow look at midday?

_____

_____

Q3 Draw arrows on the picture to show how the snake sees the egg. Then write down what happens.

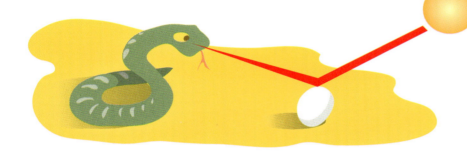

_____

_____

_____

SCIENCE FACT

You can see some amazing shadow puppets from Java at:

http://discover-indo.tierranet.com/wayang.html

Why not have a go at making some of your own?

I love scaring Sam with the long spooky shadows I make on the bedroom wall. The thing is, he's even scared of his own shadow!

Can you explain how a shadow is made?

Challenge

BRAIN TEASER

We see things as light bounces off an object and enters our eyes. Make a list of five sources of light that help us to see things.

1 _____

2 _____

3 _____

4 _____

5 _____

There are many types of force. Forces can make things move or stop moving! If an object is still, the forces are balanced. If an object starts to move, moves more quickly or slowly, stops or changes direction, we say the forces are unbalanced.

Gravity is a force. The Earth is very big, so it has a large gravitational pull. It is the force of gravity pulling us down towards the Earth that stops us from floating around.

Friction is also a force. It slows things down and can stop things from starting to move. It is friction between our shoes and the floor that stops us slipping over. When the floor is wet, friction is reduced and we slip. Friction warms things up. Think about what happens when you rub your hands together on a cold day.

Air resistance also makes things slow down. Racing cars or planes like Concord have pointed front ends, because the pointed shape cuts down on wind resistance. A big flat front end would give a large surface for the air to push back against. This would not allow the car or plane to easily travel at very high speeds.

THE FORCE IS WITH YOU

Q1 **Have a go at answering these questions.**

a What is the name of the force that makes things fall when they are dropped?

_____

b Which force heats our hands when we rub them together?

_____

c Why do you think we put down grit when the ground is icy?

_____

d Why does having a pointed front end allow a plane to travel at higher speeds?

_____

Q2 Look at these statements. Then write T in the box for the ones that are true and F for the ones that are false.

a Friction can warm things up.

b Friction makes things go faster.

c Friction makes things slow down.

d Concord has a big flat front end to cut air resistance.

e Gravity makes things fall when they are dropped.

f Gravity makes things slide about.

Q3 Draw a racing car in the box below. Label the features that will help it to travel fast. Then draw in arrows to show how forces are acting on the car.

SCIENCE FACT

Other planets, apart from the Earth, make gravity too. The Moon has a weaker gravitational pull than the Earth, because it is smaller.

I wish I lived on the Moon. Then I could bounce around like the astronauts I see on the telly! Find out how much weaker the gravitational pull of the Moon is than the Earth. You could look in books or on the Internet.

Challenge

BRAIN TEASER

Gravity makes things fall to the ground when we drop them. If we dropped an apple and a football at the same time, which would hit the ground first? Give a reason for your answer.

_____

_____

_____

_____

Do you know why we have seasons? Or day and night? It's all to do with the movement of the Earth as it spins in space! The Earth moves around the Sun once every year. The Earth turns once every 24 hours. We call this a day, but it is really a day and a night. There are 365 days in a year, plus one more in a leap year! Leap years happen because it actually takes 365 and a quarter days for the Earth to travel round, or orbit, the Sun. The Sun seems to move across the sky through the day, but really it stays where it is and the Earth moves. The spinning of the Earth makes it seem that the Sun has changed position.

The seasons are caused by the Earth tilting on its axis as it turns. Imagine a line running through the centre like a pencil stuck through an orange. As the north of the Earth tilts towards the Sun, we have spring and summer. As the north tilts away from the Sun, we have autumn and winter.

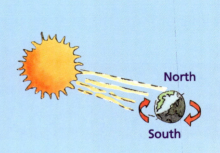

North

South

SEASON'S GREETINGS

Q1 **Fill in the gaps in the sentences, using the words in the box below.**

> day   tilts   leap   axis   Earth

SCIENCE FACT
Never look directly at the Sun, as it can damage your eyes!

a The _____ moves round the Sun.

b We have seasons because the Earth tilts on its _____ as it spins.

c There are 365 days in one year, except in a _____ year.

d The Earth turns once every _____ .

e As the Earth _____ away from the Sun, we have autumn and winter.

Q2 Look at these statements. If they are true, write T in the box. if they are false, write F.

a The seasons change because of changing tilt of the Earth as it spins in space. ☐

b The Earth is shaped like a flat disc. ☐

c The Earth moves round the sun once every week. ☐

d We have day and night because of the movement of the Earth as it spins in space. ☐

e The Earth spins on an axle. ☐

f The Earth spins on its axis. ☐

Q3 See if you can draw the sun in the correct places.

a Draw a picture of where the Sun would appear in the sky at sunrise.

b Now draw a picture of where the Sun would appear in the sky at midday.

c Finally, draw a picture of where the Sun would appear in the sky at sunset.

Sam said he wished my birthday happened on 29th February, because then he'd only have to buy me a present once every four years! Can you explain why we have leap years?

Challenge

BRAIN TEASER

Tell someone why the Sun seems to rise in the east and set in the west.

_____

_____

_____

_____

_____

MAGNETIC ATTRACTION

Not all metals are attracted to magnets. Magnets attract metals containing iron, such as steel. Strong magnets can sometimes work through materials like paper, fabric or card. It depends on the thickness of the material.

The two ends of each magnet are called poles. Magnets have a north pole and a south pole.

If you put two poles that are the same together (north + north or south + south), the magnets will push away from each other. We call this repulsion.

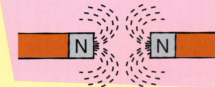

If you put two opposite poles together (north and south) the magnets will pull towards each other. We call this attraction.

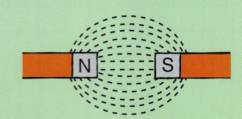

Q1 Look at the pairs of bar magnets. Write *attract* or *repel* in the boxes to show what will happen. Then finish off the two sentences.

a

b

c

d

e Attraction happens when _____

_____

f Repulsion happens when _____

_____

Q2 True or false? Mark the sentences T or F.

a If you put two north poles together, they will repel each other. ☐

b If you put a north and south pole together, they will repel each other. ☐

c All metals are attracted to a magnet. ☐

d Metals containing iron are attracted to a magnet. ☐

e If you put two north poles together, they will be attracted to each other. ☐

Q3 Have a go at answering these questions.

a Which materials are attracted to a magnet? _____

b What will happen if a south pole and a north pole are put together?

_____

c Will two north poles together *attract* or *repel*? _____

d Which combinations of poles will be attracted to one another?

_____

I don't know why they say opposites attract. I'm about as different to Mel as you can get and I never feel attracted to spend time in her company! Make sure you know which poles are attracted to each other and which repel. Draw a picture to remind yourself.

Challenge

BRAIN TEASER

Design a game to explain to a young child which things are attracted to a magnet. Explain how your game works here. (You may need to use an extra sheet of paper.)

_____

_____

_____

_____

_____

We use electricity to power lights, lamps, TVs, computers, games consoles and toys. Some use mains electricity, which is the electricity that we use by putting a plug into a wall socket. It can be dangerous, so never poke anything into a socket or use plugs and switches with wet hands because you could get an electric shock.

The electricity that powers toys using a battery is perfectly safe. This is the type of electricity you use in school. Batteries create electricity when the chemicals inside the battery react with each other. Electricity is not stored in an ordinary battery. The chemicals inside react with one another to generate power.

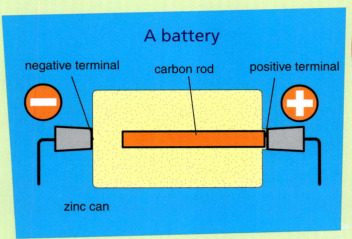

A battery

negative terminal   carbon rod   positive terminal

zinc can

For electricity to flow round a circuit, the components – such as wires, bulb and battery (or cell) – must be joined correctly. If a circuit is broken, the bulb will not light.

DOING THE CIRCUIT

Q1 Draw a picture of a circuit that will make a bulb light. Then explain how the bulb lights.

Q2 Circuit components all have special functions. Draw the component next to the description.

a Pushes the electric current through the wires.

b Gives off light when electricity passes through it.

c Makes a noise when electricity passes through it.

d Links together different components (parts) in a circuit.

e Can be used to break the flow of electricity, to turn the bulb 'on' and 'off'.

DOING THE CIRCUIT

SCIENCE FACT
Never try to open, break or burn a battery because the chemicals inside can burn your skin.

Q3 Name four things in your home that use mains electricity and four things that use batteries.

mains electricity

a _____

b _____

c _____

d _____

battery electricity

e _____

f _____

g _____

h _____

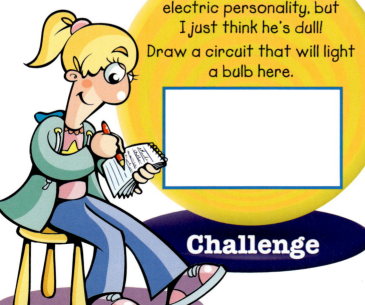

Sam thinks he has an electric personality, but I just think he's *dull!*

Draw a circuit that will light a bulb here.

Challenge

BRAIN TEASER

Explain how a battery works. How does it produce electricity?

_____

_____

_____

_____

_____

TEST PRACTICE

1 What would happen to a plant growing without enough water?

_____

_____

2 What would happen to a plant growing in a dark cupboard?

_____

_____

3 Plants

Draw the part of the plant next to its function.

attracts insects with its scent and colour | holds the plant in the ground | makes food using sunlight

4 Why do some plants have feathery flowers, like grasses?

_____

_____

5 Sort these creatures into the two groups below.

cat   newt   parrot   tiger   pigeon   snake   whale   pig

lays eggs   **does not lay eggs**

_____   _____

_____   _____

_____   _____

_____   _____

6 How else could you sort the animals in question 5 into groups?

_____

_____

7 Name the seven processes that show us things are alive.

a _____

b _____

c _____

d _____

e _____

f _____

g _____

8 Draw these life cycles in order.

a hen   egg   chick

b tadpole   frogspawn   frog

c child   baby   adult

d Which life cycle shows a metamorphosis? What does this mean?

_____

_____

_____

9 Who lives where? Draw a line to match the animal to the habitat.

a parrot   antarctic

b sea anemone   jungle

c camel   seashore

d penguin   desert

10 Circle the foods in each pair that are the heathy choice.

a Peaches or peach flan?

b Lemons or lemonade?

c Water or sweetened fizzy drink?

11 Answer these questions.

a What is plaque?

_____

b How can it damage teeth?

_____

c What is tooth enamel?

_____

d What is dentine?

_____

12 Look at these statements. Write T in the box if they are true and F if they are false.

a All metals are attracted to magnets. ☐

b Metals containing iron are attracted to magnets. ☐

c North and south magnet poles would be attracted to each other. ☐

d North and south magnet poles would repel each other. ☐

13 a Why are racing cars designed with pointed front ends?

_____

_____

b Which force makes things fall when they are dropped?

_____

c Is there more gravity on the Earth or the Moon? Explain how you know and why this is the case.

_____

_____

_____

14 Tick which recycling bank you would put these things into.

	bottle bank	can bank	paper bank	plastic bank
a Newspaper	☐	☐	☐	☐
b Glass bottle	☐	☐	☐	☐
c Plastic milk bottle	☐	☐	☐	☐
d Jam jar	☐	☐	☐	☐
e Magazine	☐	☐	☐	☐
f Bubble wrap packaging	☐	☐	☐	☐

15 Choose the best material from the list below to make each object. Then explain your choice.

cardboard   wood   glass   plastic   paper

a Chair: _____

b Doll: _____

c Comic: _____

d Window: _____

e Box: _____

16 Mark in the boxes which changes are reversible.

a An icicle melts and turns into water.

b Chocolate melts and changes from a solid to a liquid.

c Pancake batter is fried.

d Steam cools on a window and turns into water.

17 Draw the arrows to show how the boy sees the crab.

18 a Draw a set of magnets with their poles arranged so that they repel one another. Don't forget to draw in the lines of repulsion.

b Draw a set of magnets with their poles arranged so that they are attracted to one another. Don't forget to draw in the lines of attraction.

19 Which of these objects use mains electricity?

20 Tick the circuits that would not light the bulb.

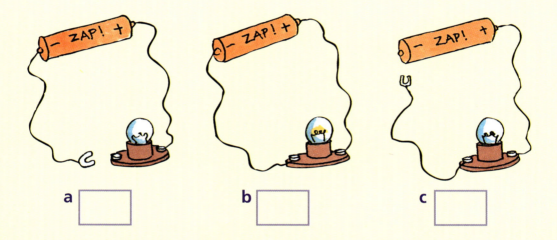

a ☐   b ☐   c ☐

21 Which circuit component:

a pushes electricity through a circuit

_____

b breaks the flow of electricity in a circuit

_____

c lights up as electricity flows through it

_____

Pages 4–5

Q1 a F   b T   c F   d T
    e F   f T

Q2 b should be ticked.

Q3 1 brown   4 light
    2 dry   5 healthy
    3 yellow

Brain teaser
The article must include that a plant needs plenty of light and water. An ideal place for a plant would be on a light window sill.

Pages 6–7

Q1 a T   b T   c T   d F
    e T

Q2 a root   d pollinated
    b sunlight   e germinated
    c water

Q3 Dandelion seed – b   Coconut – a
    Holly berry – c   Burr – d

Brain teaser
1 Diagram of a plant pollinated by an insect, i.e. rose, daffodil.
2 Diagram of a plant pollinated by the wind i.e. grass.

Pages 8–9

Q1

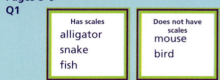

Has scales	Does not have scales
alligator	mouse
snake	bird
fish	

Q2

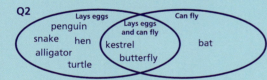

Kestrel and butterfly are in both groups.

Q3 a reptile   b flowering plant
    c bird   d insect

Brain teaser
A variety of answers, one could be:

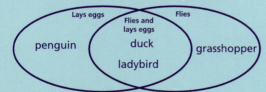

Pages 10–11

Q1 b, c, e, g, i, j, and k should be ticked.

Q2 a T   b F   c F   d T
    e T   f T

Q3 tree, cat, bird, daffodil, butterfly, grass, bushes

Brain teaser
1 breathe   2 waste
3 grow   4 living

Pages 12–13

Q1

Natural	Made by people
wool	plastic
wood	metal
stone	glass
chalk	polystyrene
feathers	

Q2 a jumper   d steel nail
    b china bowl   e chair
    c glass window

Q3 a ring   d carved chair
    b china mug   e glass vase
    c woollen coat

Brain teaser
The following should be circled:

Pages 14–15

Q1 a rubbish   b discarded
    c recycled   d urban

Q2

Answers will vary, but may include:
Yoghurt pot – for planting small seedlings.
Newspaper – recycled to make pulp.

Q3 a jam jar, glass bottle
    b newspaper, comic
    c drinks can, baked bean tin
    d banana skin, apple core

Brain teaser

Reuse	Recycle
cottage cheese pot	comic
glass milk bottle	lemonade can
	bean tin

Pages 16–17

Q1 shore crab; camel; raccoon;
    A variety including:
    a hedgehog   b rabbit

Q2 Wall = snail
    Pond = tadpole
    Flowerbed = butterfly
    Leafpile = earwig

Q3 a slug   b newt
    c butterfly

Brain teaser
Must describe trees it lives in; that it eats and hoards nuts; where it finds food.

Pages 18–19

Q1 a bones   d invertebrates
    b support   e joints
    c muscles

Q2 a ribs **b** backbone
c skull **d** pelvis

Q3

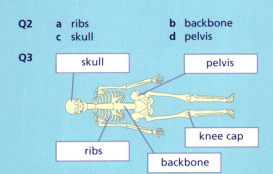

skull

pelvis

ribs

knee cap

backbone

Brain teaser

1 Vertebrates – animals with backbones, for example dogs.
4 Invertebrates – animals without backbones, for example worms.

Pages 20–21

Q1 a chewing **d** canines
b incisors **e** decay
c carnivores **f** herbivores

Q2 a F **b** F **c** F **d** T
e F **f** T

Q3

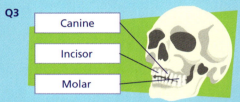

Canine

Incisor

Molar

a for tearing meat
b for cutting food
c for grinding food

Brain teaser

1 For grinding the grass they eat.
2 Because some humans eat meat and vegetables.

Pages 22–23

Q1 Example drawings are:

carbohydrates

vitamins and minerals

fat

fibre

protein

Q2 a Because our bodies are mainly made of water.
b Because they contain vitamins, minerals and fibre.
c To keep our teeth and bones healthy.

Q3 A variety of answers: must include something containing protein, carbohydrates, fibre (may have a fat in it), plus either water, milk or a fruit juice.

Brain teaser

A variety of answers are possible, including:

Main course: wholemeal cheese or salad sandwiches or wholemeal bread toast with beans on top.

Dessert: Fruit salad or yoghurt.

Drink: Water or juice.

Pages 24–25

Q1 a pump **d** arteries
b veins **e** bacteria
c platelets **f** microscopic

Q2 a T **b** F **c** T **d** F
e T **f** F

Q3

heartbeat

X

time

Brain teaser

1 red blood cell **2** platelet
3 white blood cell

Pages 26–27

Q1 Frog, butterfly, ladybird and dragonfly should be circled.

Q2

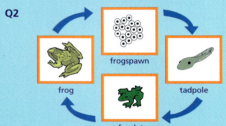

frogspawn

frog

tadpole

froglet

Q3 First box should contain a picture of a baby (c). Second box should contain a picture of a toddler (e). Third box should contain a picture of a little girl (f). Fourth box should contain a picture of a teenager (b). Fifth box should contain a picture of an adult mum (d). Sixth box should contain a picture of an elderly grandma (a).

Brain teaser

A variety of answers are possible, including:
1 hedgehog **2** rabbit
3 tiger **4** dog

Pages 28–29

Q1 a trousers **d** walls
b window **e** doll
c box

Q2 a metal **d** plastic
b wool **e** stone
c paper

Q3

Transparent	Opaque
glass	cardboard
clear plastic ruler	milk
water	mirror
clear plastic bag	wooden tray

Brain teaser

A variety of answers including;

1 Window: glass, because it is transparent, you can see through it and it lets in light.

Pages 30–31

Q1
a solid   d gas
b liquid   e solid
c gas   f liquid

Q2
a solid, liquid   b gas, liquid
c liquid, solid

Q3
a reversible   d reversible
b reversible   e reversible
c irreversible

Brain teaser

1 solid   2 solid, liquid
3 liquid   4 solid

Pages 32–33

Q1
a sound   d vibrations
b waves   e decibels
c eardrums

Q2
a A, because it is closest to the boy.

Q3
a very loud sounds   b infection
c poking them

Q4 Wear ear plugs.

Brain teaser

A variety of answers, including:
1 roadworks
2 factory machinery
3 an aircraft taking off
4 loud music at a rock concert.

Pages 34–35

Q1
a F   b F   c T   d F
e F   f F   g T

Q2

a It is long because of the Sun's low position.
b It would be short and fat.

Q3

The light comes from the Sun, bounces off the egg and enters the snake's eyes.

Brain teaser

A variety of answers, including:
1 Sun   4 torches
2 street lamp   5 fire
3 candle flame

Pages 36–37

Q1
a gravity
b friction
c to create more friction
d because it cuts down on air resistance

Q2
a T   b F   c T   d F
e T   f F

Q3

Brain teaser

They would both hit the floor at the same time because the Earth's gravitational force would pull them both down to Earth at the same speed.

Pages 38–39

Q1
a Earth   b axis   c leap   d day
e tilts

Q2
a T   b F   c F   d T
e F   f T

Q3

Brain teaser

Because the Earth spins on its axis and as the Earth spins away from the Sun it spins to the west.

Pages 40–41

Q1
a repel   b attract   c repel   d attract
e Two magnets with opposite poles pulls them towards each other.
f Two magnets with the same poles push away from each other.

Q2
a T   b F   c F   d T
e F

Q3
a metals containing iron
b They will be attracted to each other.
c repel
d north and south or south and north

Brain teaser

Any game that shows young children the rules of magnets.

Pages 42–43

Q1 An example drawing would be:

Q2 **a**   **d**

b   **e**

c

Q3 A variety of answers including:

Mains electricity	Battery electricity
reading lamp	personal stereo
kettle	torch
TV	watch
video player	some calculators

Brain teaser

When chemicals inside a battery react with each other, they create electricity.

Pages 44–50 Test Practice

1 It would dry up.

2 It would turn yellow.

3

attracts insects with its scent and colour | holds the plant in the ground | makes food using sunlight

4 To release pollen into the wind.

5
Lays eggs	Does not lay eggs
newt	cat
parrot	tiger
pigeon	whale
snake	pig

6 A variety of answers are possible, including: flies and cannot fly.

7 **a** movement
b respiration
c reproduction
d feeds
e sensitivity
f growth and change
g getting rid of waste

8 **a**

b

b

d B shows a metamorphosis. This means the baby looks completely different to the adult.

9 **a** parrot – jungle
b sea anemone – seashore
c camel – desert
d penguin – antarctic

10 **a** peaches **b** lemons **c** water

11 **a** When bacteria breaks down food into sugars. This sticky substance is called plaque.
b It causes tooth decay.
c The hard white casing around your teeth.
d The soft material inside your teeth.

12 **a** F **b** T **c** T **d** F

13 **a** So they cut through air resistance.
b Gravity.
c The Earth, because it is larger than the the Moon.

14 **a** paper bank **d** bottle bank
b bottle bank **e** paper bank
c plastic bank **f** plastic bank

15 **a** Wood, because it is strong.
b Plastic, because it can be moulded into lots of shapes.
c Paper, because it can be printed on easily. It is light, easy to use and cheap.
d Glass, becuase it is transparent and lets light through.
e Cardboard, because it is light but strong.

16 a, b and d are reversible.

17

18 **a** **b**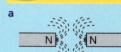

19

20 a and **c** will not light the bulb.

21 **a** battery **b** switch
c bulb

REALLY USEFUL WORDS

Adaptation The way in which plants and animals change over time to cope with the conditions in their environment.

Air resistance This can make things slow down, depending on the shape of the thing the air is moving over. A big, flat shape will resist lots of air.

Artery The blood vessel that carries blood away from the heart.

Bacteria Tiny germs that can make us ill. Another name is *micro organism*.

Carbohydrate A food group that provides energy that the body can easily use. Pasta, wholemeal bread and cereals are rich in carbohydrates.

Canine teeth The sharp teeth used by carnivores to kill and eat their food.

Carnivore An animal that eats only meat is called a carnivore. An example would be a tiger.

Db The symbol that stands for the unit that measures sound – decibels.

Decibels The unit used to measure sound.

Fats These are stored in the body. When the body needs energy, it uses some of these fat supplies.

Fibre Found in foods such as vegetables and wholemeal bread. It helps to keep the digestive system working properly.

Friction The force that happens when two surfaces rub together. Friction stops us from slipping over.

Germination When a seed starts to grow, it has germinated. We call the process germination. The root grows like a white thread first.

Gravity The force that makes things fall to the ground. The Earth is huge, so it creates a strong gravitational pull.

Habitat Where a creature or plant lives, such as a desert, wood, seashore or jungle.

Herbivore Animals that only eat plants and no meat. An example is a rabbit.

Incisors The large front teeth, used for cropping and cutting food.

Internal organs These are the parts of our bodies such as the heart and the lungs. We cannot see them because they are inside our bodies and therefore internal.

Irreversible change A change that cannot be changed back to the original. A piece of wood being burned is an example. (See Reversible changes.)

Metamorphosis When a creature goes through a complete change as it grows. Frogs, ladybirds, butterflies and dragonflies all go through metamorphosis.

Molars Large teeth used for grinding food.

Oscilloscope An instrument used for measuring sound waves.

Platelets Tiny fragments in the blood that help it to clot, so we form scabs when we cut ourselves.

Pollinate This happens when pollen is taken from a flower to help make more seeds somewhere else. Pollen can be carried by insects or the wind.

Protein Our bodies need protein to help them grow and repair.

Recycle Using waste to make something else. For example, old newspapers could be used to make pulp, which is then made into cardboard.

Red blood cells Cells in the blood that carry oxygen and dissolved nutrients from food around the body. They also carry carbon dioxide back to the lungs so we can breathe it out.

Reversible change A change that can be reversed, such as melted butter being put into the fridge and going hard again.

Veins The blood vessels that carry blood to the heart.

Venn diagram A diagram that uses circles to sort things into sets.

Virus A tiny micro organism that can cause illnesses like 'flu.

White blood cells These blood cells fight bacteria and viruses to keep us healthy.